THE
gluten, wheat, and dairy free
COOKBOOK

NICOLA GRAIMES

p

This is a Parragon Publishing Book
This edition published in 2005

Parragon Publishing
Queen Street House
4 Queen Street
Bath
BA1 1HE
UK

Designed and produced by
THE BRIDGEWATER BOOK COMPANY

Nutritional Analyses and Facts: *Charlotte Watts*
Photography: *Clive Bozzard-Hill*
Home Economist: *Philippa Vanstone*
Stylist: *Angela Macfarlane*

The publishers would like to thank the following companies for the loan
of props: *Dartington Crystal, Marlux Mills, Maxwell & Williams, Lifestyle Collections,
Viners and Oneida, and John Lewis.*

Printed in China

Copyright © Parragon 2004

ISBN: 1-40543-686-7

NOTES FOR THE READER

This book uses imperial, metric, or US cup measurements. Follow the same units of measurement throughout; do not mix imperial and metric. All spoon measurements are level, unless otherwise stated: teaspoons are assumed to be 5 ml and tablespoons are assumed to be 15 ml.

Individual vegetables such as potatoes are medium and pepper is freshly ground black pepper.

Some of the recipes require stock. If you use commercially made bouillon granules or cubes, these can have a relatively high salt content, so do not add any further salt. If you make your own stock, keep the fat and salt content to a minimum. Don't sauté the vegetables before simmering—just simmer the vegetables, herbs, and meat, poultry, or fish in water and strain. Meat and poultry stocks should be strained, cooled, and refrigerated before use so that the fat from the meat rises to the top and solidifies—it can then be easily removed and this reduces the saturated fat content of the meal. Homemade stocks should be stored in the refrigerator and used within two days, or frozen in usable portions and labeled.

Cooking times may vary as a result of the type of oven used. Ovens should be preheated to the specified temperature. If using a fan-assisted oven, check the manufacturer's instructions for adjusting the time and temperature.

The values of the nutritional analysis for each recipe refer to a single serving, or a single slice where relevant. They do not include the serving suggestion. Where a range of portions is given the nutritional analysis figure refers to the mid-range figure. The calorific value given is in KCal (Kilocalories). The carbohydrate figure includes starches and sugars, with the sugar value then given separately. The fat figure is likewise the total fat, with the saturated part then given separately.

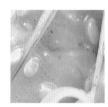

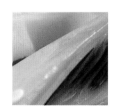

     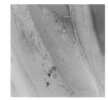

contents

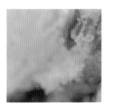    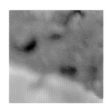 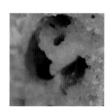

Introduction

A Fresh Start

Approximately two percent of people in the US are said to suffer from some form of food allergy, and two of the most common food groups that may cause an adverse reaction are grains and dairy products. A gluten-, wheat-, and dairy-free diet was once regarded as nutrient-deficient, restrictive, and difficult to follow, but it is now much easier to adopt, thanks to a growing acceptance and understanding of these dietary problems by the medical profession, along with the wide availability of so many alternative ingredients. If you have a food allergy or intolerance, it need not spoil your pleasure in cooking and eating. Instead, see it as an opportunity to experiment with new recipes and previously untried ingredients.

Allergy or Intolerance?

A food allergy occurs when the immune system overreacts to a normally harmless substance in a food by producing antibodies. This type of reaction often runs in families and can strike at any age. It may also cause a wide range of symptoms from a runny nose and headache to a potentially life-threatening reaction suffered by those who are allergic to nuts, for example.

Somewhat confusingly, if you test negatively for an allergy but still react to certain foods, then you may have what is controversially called an intolerance. An intolerance is often caused by a digestive problem.

What is a Gluten Allergy or Intolerance?

Gluten is a protein found in many cereal grains, including wheat, barley, rye, triticale, spelt, kamut, and oats, and it is this substance that can cause a severe reaction in susceptible individuals. This reaction is known as celiac disease. Celiac disease is an inflammatory condition of the gastrointestinal tract. It is characterized by a flattening or wasting away of the villi—threadlike projections that line the intestines. The role of the villi is to absorb essential nutrients freed by the digestive process, and it is this process that is compromised in those with celiac disease, causing among other symptoms malnutrition and weight loss.

Celiac disease used to be rare and was once seen as a condition exclusive to childhood, but doctors now recognize that the disorder can affect people of all ages. While it may be present from birth and often runs in families, celiac disease often remains undetected until adulthood. In the US, about one in 2,000–2,500 people are believed to be affected by the life-long condition, yet this figure may be much higher due to many cases remaining undiagnosed.

What are the Symptoms?

The symptoms of celiac disease are varied, ranging from a mild reaction to chronic illness, which can make diagnosis difficult. The most common symptoms include poor absorption of nutrients, particularly iron and folate, weight loss, mouth ulcers, nausea, bloating, extreme fatigue, lethargy, diarrhea, flatulence, and abdominal discomfort. In babies, celiac disease will probably not become apparent until weaning, when gluten-containing foods are introduced. The infant will then typically develop pale, offensive-smelling stools, lethargy, vomiting, diarrhea, irritability, and a failure to grow properly.

How is it Diagnosed?

If gluten intolerance is suspected, a blood test is carried out to confirm the presence of antibodies and vitamin and mineral deficiencies. The blood tests are not 100 percent accurate, so confirmation of a diagnosis is usually determined by a biopsy. Generally performed by a gastroenterologist, a sample is taken from the lining of the small bowel using an endoscope, which will confirm the diagnosis of celiac disease. It is recommended that you follow a normal diet containing gluten for six weeks prior to the blood test and biopsy to achieve accurate results.

What is the Treatment?

Once diagnosis has been confirmed, it is advisable to discuss the next step with a dietician or doctor before embarking on an elimination diet. The only treatment necessary to return the intestine to normal is to follow a strict gluten-free diet, eliminating the consumption of the cereal grains in question and any manufactured foods containing them, sometimes with a vitamin and mineral supplement. However, there is new research to suggest that some individuals may be able to tolerate small amounts of oats (less than scant $5/8$ cup a day) in their diets, but it is advisable to consult your doctor or dietician before including oats in your diet and people with severe celiac disease should avoid them altogether.

There are two forms of gluten foods: the first is the obvious bread, pasta, cookies, and pastries, while the second type relates to hidden gluten found in many manufactured foods. This could be wheat flour used as a binder or filler in foods as diverse as packaged soups and bottled sauces. Those with celiac disease need to become avid readers of nutritional information given on food labels to check for hidden sources of gluten.

What is a Wheat Allergy?

Wheat forms a major part of most people's diets, yet it is also a common allergen. The symptoms of wheat allergy or intolerance are varied and may include itchy, sore eyes; runny nose, sinusitis, or sneezing; earache or ringing in the ears; headaches, migraine, or dizziness; sore throats, bad breath, cough, or mouth ulcers; skin rashes, acne, eczema, or inexplicable bruising; stomach cramps, bloating, nausea, constipation, or flatulence; as well as anxiety, depression, poor concentration, or aggressive behavior. Individuals who are allergic to wheat may be able to tolerate other grains, including those that contain gluten, such as rye, barley, and oats.

Dermatitis Herpetiformis

This relatively rare skin disease is caused, like celiac disease, by a sensitivity to gluten. It is characterized by an itchy rash that usually occurs on the elbows, buttocks, and knees, although any area of the skin may be affected. Dermatitis herpetiformis is slightly more common in adult males than females and usually appears between the ages of 15 and 40, although it may occur at any age.

Am I Missing Out on Nutrients?

Before diagnosis, celiacs have a problem absorbing nutrients from their diet, yet when gluten is excluded from the diet and as long as the sufferer eats a wide and varied diet, the body is in a better position to absorb nutrients from food. If you have cut out foods containing wheat and gluten, you may be concerned that you are not getting enough fiber. This is not a problem as long as you eat plenty of fruit and vegetables, other gluten-free grains, beans, lentils, and brown rice. Other nutrients found in wheat, barley, oats, and rye include:
• zinc, found in nuts, seafood, oysters, whole-grains, beans, seeds, liver, and meat.
• vitamin B_1 (thiamine), found in whole-grains, nuts, beans, meat, and brewer's yeast.
• vitamin B_2 (riboflavin), found in eggs, yeast, green vegetables, pepitas, and variety meats.
• vitamin B_3 (niacin), found in eggs, whole-grains, nuts, seafood, figs, prunes, and variety meats.
• vitamin E, found in avocados, soybeans, dark green vegetables, eggs, nuts, and vegetable oils.

What is a Dairy Allergy or Intolerance?

Dairy products, especially those derived from cow's milk, are a common allergen. Milk, cheese, cream, fromage frais, crème fraîche, yogurt, and butter are obvious culprits, yet dairy products are found in many processed foods. A dairy allergy or intolerance usually manifests itself in childhood. A baby who is often sick, has colic, or fails to thrive may be showing symptoms of a dairy allergy or intolerance, while weaning an infant too young may also encourage an allergic reaction. Thankfully, many children grow out of such allergies or intolerances by the age of five.

A reaction to dairy products is often due to lactose intolerance. This is when the body cannot produce an enzyme called lactase, which is necessary for the digestion of the natural sugar in milk, lactose. Those with lactose intolerance may be able to tolerate small amounts of dairy foods such as skim milk (rather than whole milk), yogurt, or goat milk, which are easier to digest. Although relatively unusual, some people may also be intolerant to the protein in dairy products, which causes similar side effects as lactose intolerance.

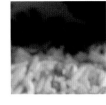

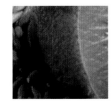

What are the Symptoms?

An allergy or intolerance to dairy products can provoke a wide range of symptoms, the most common being asthma, eczema, digestive problems, irritable bowel syndrome (IBS), rashes, sinus problems, including rhinitis, as well as migraines, and headaches. If an individual does not produce the enzyme lactase, the lactose cannot be digested, which means that it passes unchanged into the large intestine where it is fermented by bacteria, causing bloating, stomach pains and diarrhea. There is also growing evidence that child-onset diabetes is caused by dairy intolerance.

How is it Diagnosed?

It can be difficult to detect the presence of a dairy allergy or intolerance since symptoms may arise as soon as the problem food is eaten or may manifest themselves hours later. Symptoms may also vary depending on the individual. There are a number of tests now available to detect allergies, including the RAST test, which measures the amount of immunoglobulin E antibodies (IgE) a person has to a specific substance, as well as the skin-prick test, whereby a small scratch is made by a pin carrying a suspect food and any reaction such as redness or swelling is monitored. Naturopaths also offer hair analysis and blood tests with varying success.

What is the Treatment?

A food exclusion diet, whereby offending foods are removed from the diet, is not only the most effective way of detecting the presence of a food intolerance or allergy but the most obvious way of eliminating symptoms. However, it can be a long and laborious process, which normally begins by keeping a detailed food diary. It is always important to consult a doctor or dietician before eliminating foods from your diet, who will be able to devise a nutritious, balanced, alternative diet.

When following a dairy exclusion diet, it is important to check the nutritional information on the labels of all foods and supplements before buying, since some artificial sweeteners and food supplements may also contain dairy-derived ingredients. Medicines can also have a dairy-derived content.

Am I Missing Out on Nutrients?

Milk and dairy products are a useful source of protein, zinc, calcium, and vitamin B_{12}, so it is important to substitute these foods with others containing these nutrients. There are many nondairy alternatives to milk that provide calcium, namely green leafy vegetables, sesame seeds, canned fish such as sardines and pilchards, white bread, apricots, soy milk, molasses, nuts, seafood, cereals, seeds, beans, and soy products, while this group of foods also supplies valuable amounts of zinc. Vitamin B_{12} is provided by meat, fortified breakfast cereals, soy milk, and yeast extract.

What Can I Eat?

If you are new to gluten-, wheat-, and dairy-free cooking, understanding and remembering the ingredients that you can and can't eat can be quite daunting at first. It may require a total rethink of your repertoire of recipes and will undoubtedly demand a complete clean-out of your pantry, refrigerator, and freezer. Try not to feel restricted or frightened by your new diet but regard it as the chance to explore a range of new foods, flavors, and dishes. If catering for someone else, be reassured that cooking meals that are gluten-, wheat-, and dairy-free is not difficult and they can be enjoyed by everyone in the family.

Checking the ingredients on food labels will need to become second nature, since a surprising number of foods contain wheat, gluten, and dairy products, along with their derivatives. The most common dairy foods you need to avoid are cheese, cream, butter, milk, ice cream, and yogurt. Foods such as pasta, noodles, bread, cakes, cookies, pastries, and pies are usually made with wheat, while barley, rye, and oats also contain gluten. You will also need to watch out for canned soups, ready-prepared sauces and meals, as well as desserts, which may have added gluten or dairy products. Fillers, thickeners, and binders are often wheat-based.

There are two forms of exclusion diet. The first relies on individuals suspecting which foods are causing a problem and eliminating them from their diet for a designated period of time to see if symptoms improve. The problem foods are then reintroduced to see if the symptoms recur. The second type of exclusion diet begins by eating a restricted diet based on a few foods that are highly unlikely to cause an allergic reaction. Foods are then reintroduced, one by one, on a gradual basis. If a food causes a reaction, it is subsequently eliminated from the diet. Obviously, this type of exclusion diet can take some time to complete.

Scientists are currently working on a new method of treating allergies or intolerances, but it is not as yet widely available. This involves administering tiny doses of an allergen with a naturally occurring enzyme through injection to desensitize its side effects. Those who are lactose intolerant may also take the enzyme lactase, which gives the body a helping hand in breaking down lactose in dairy foods.

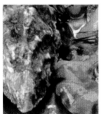

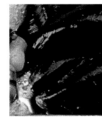

A Gluten-, Wheat-, and Dairy-free Diet

Let's forget about what you can't eat and concentrate on the wide variety of delicious alternatives. If you eat a varied, balanced diet including the following food groups, you should get all the nutrients you need:

• Meat, fish, poultry, or vegetarian alternatives

Fresh, frozen, cured, and canned meat, fish, and poultry are suitable but avoid those with a crumb coating or stuffing and check out processed pies, sausages, and burgers. Some brands of meat-free sausages and burgers are suitable but double-check the label before buying. Tofu is a nutritious, lowfat, vegetarian source of protein.

• Fruit and vegetables

Fresh, frozen, dried, or canned (in brine, juice, syrup, water, or oil) are suitable. Potatoes make a useful alternative accompaniment to wheat-based foods such as pasta or noodles.

• Nuts and seeds

There is a wide range of ground, milled, and whole nuts and seeds to choose from, which are an excellent source of protein as well as vitamins and minerals. Only buy from stores with a high turnover of stock to ensure freshness. Nut butters (cashew, peanut, hazelnut) are also suitable. Avoid dry-roasted nuts.

• Beans and lentils

Dried, fresh, and canned (in brine, water, or oil) beans and lentils are a lowfat source of protein, fiber, vitamins, and minerals.

• Eggs

Avoid Scotch eggs due to their crumb coating.

• Drinks

Coffee, tea, herbal infusions, pure fruit juices, and water are all suitable. Check cocoa, malted drinks, beer, spirits, and wine for gluten, wheat, and dairy additives.

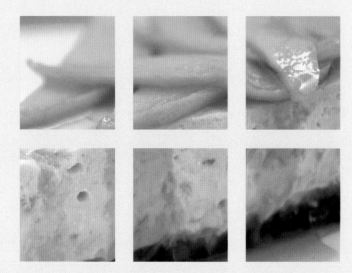

• Grains and cereals

There is now a wide range of alternatives to wheat and other gluten-containing grains, flakes, and flours, including corn, buckwheat, millet, hominy grits, quinoa, sago, tapioca, rice, yam, gram or chickpea flour, cornmeal, arrowroot, cornstarch, sorghum flour, potato flour, carob flour, teff flour, soy flour, sweet chestnut flour, and yellow split dried field pea flour. Breakfast cereals include some brands of corn flakes and granola, puffed rice, and rice crispies. For more information about the different types of grain, see below.

• Dairy-free alternatives

Soy, nut, rice, pea, quinoa, and oat milk (some celiacs may be able to tolerate the latter) are useful alternatives to dairy milk. Nondairy soft and hard cheeses include alternatives to mozzarella, Edam, Gouda, Stilton, cream cheese, Parmesan, and Cheddar. Soy yogurt, cream, and ice cream are also available.

• Fats and oils

Look for dairy-free margarine (make sure it does not contain wheat germ oil) and olive, vegetable, and nut oils.

• Pasta and noodles

There is a wide range of gluten-, wheat-, and dairy-free alternatives available made from corn, buckwheat, rice, and millet flour, either used in combination or singly. Make sure that noodles and pasta do not contain added wheat flour, starch, or binders.

• Chocolate and sweet foods

Look for semisweet, good-quality chocolate without added dairy products. Jellies, honey, marmalade, and maple syrup are all suitable.

• Gluten-free grains

There is a large variety of grains and cereals, whole, flaked, or ground, to choose from that are both versatile and nutritious. The following are the most readily available gluten-free alternatives:

•Rice

This staple food for over half the world's population comes in many guises, from the sticky Japanese sushi rice to slender, fragrant basmati. For the gluten-free diet, this versatile grain offers a number of culinary possibilities, both sweet and savory. It is impossible to create the perfect creamy risotto without using a specific type of fat, short-grain rice such as carnaroli or vialone nano, while Valencia rice is essential when making Spanish paella. Then there are rice flakes, which can be added to granola, cookies, and desserts; rice bran, a high-fiber addition to breads and cakes; as well as rice flour, often used to make sticky Asian cakes and candies, and a common addition to gluten-free all-purpose and self-rising flours.

•Buckwheat

Despite its name, buckwheat is not a type of wheat. The triangular-shaped grain is available toasted (kasha) or untoasted. The flour is used in Japan to make soba noodles, in Italy to make pasta, and in Eastern Europe and Russia to make small pancakes called blinis. The flour has a grayish tinge and can be mixed with other kinds of gluten-free flour to give a lighter color and texture. Buckwheat flakes make a nutritious addition to granola. A complete protein, buckwheat also contains rutin, said to increase circulation and reduce high blood pressure.

•Millet

Known as the queen of grains, millet once rivaled barley as the staple food of Europe. It can be cooked in the same way as rice but is best dry-roasted first to enhance its mild flavor.

It is good served with stews or as a base for pilafs, porridge, and milk puddings. The tiny, round grain can also be flaked or ground into flour. Millet has antifungal properties and is said to be good for candida overgrowth. It is also easily digested and beneficial for the stomach, spleen, and pancreas.

•Quinoa

The "mother grain" of the Incas, quinoa has the highest protein content of any grain, is very high in calcium and a good source of iron, B vitamins, and vitamin E. The small, beadlike grains have a mild flavor and firm texture and make a good base for pilafs, bakes, tabbouleh (see page 35), and stuffings. It is cooked in the same way as rice. It can also be ground into flour or made into a milk.

•Amaranth

This much underrated grain contains more calcium than milk and is therefore useful for those on a dairy-free diet. Highly nutritious, amaranth is a tiny, pale grain with a strong, distinctive, nutty flavor. It can be used in stews and soups or ground into flour to make bread, cakes, and pastries. Since it has an intense flavor, it is best combined with other more neutral flours and grains. Native to Mexico, amaranth is unusual in that its leaves can also be eaten cooked or raw.

•Corn

Also known as maize, this grain comes in yellow, blue, red, and black varieties and is an indispensable addition to the gluten-free kitchen. It is a very versatile grain, with many uses. Cornmeal can be used to make bread, desserts, dumplings, or a thick savory porridge. Once cooked, cornmeal can be spread into an even layer, left to cool, then cut into slices and pan-fried, broiled, or griddled to make a base for bruschetta, or it can be served as an accompaniment to soups and stews. Cornmeal comes in various grades, ranging from fine to coarse, which can take from 5–45 minutes to cook. Corn flour or "masa harina" is made from the cooked whole grain, which is ground into flour and used to make the Mexican flat bread called tortilla. Cornstarch is a fine white powder and makes a useful thickener for sauces and soups.

Ready-made Gluten- and Wheat-free Foods

Many supermarkets now dedicate a special area to their range of gluten- and wheat-free foods, which may encompass anything from special flours, cookies, breads, pizza bases, and pasta to cakes, bread mixes, crispbreads, and breakfast cereals. Mail order and healthfood stores are also a good source.

When using gluten-free flour (both all-purpose and self-rising), it is important to follow the manufacturer's instructions since they don't necessarily perform in the same way as wheat flour.

Watch out for ...

Sources of wheat and gluten are not always easy to spot on food labels. If you notice any of the following, it is wise to check with the manufacturer: modified starch, whole-grain, starch, cereal, cereal protein, cornstarch, edible starch, food starch, binder, binding, vegetable protein, thickening or thickener, rusk, and monosodium glutamate.

Also avoid ...

Wheat berries, wheat bran, wheat flour, bulgur wheat, durum wheat, couscous, semolina, seitan, wheat germ, cracked wheat, pearl barley, barley flakes, pot barley, barley meal, rye in various forms, oats, oatmeal, oat germ, pinhead oatmeal, oat bran, spelt, triticale, and kamut.

Be aware ...

That the following may contain gluten: baking powder, gravy powder, spices, ready-ground pepper, shredded suet, mustard, bouillon granules and cubes, salad dressings, soy sauce (tamari is wheat-free), sausages, burgers, pies, ready-prepared meals, pâtés, crumb- or batter-coated fish and other foods, malt vinegar, yogurt, chilled desserts, cheese spreads, corn flakes, beer, malted-milk drinks, and dry-roasted nuts.

Alternatives to Dairy Foods

It is now easy to find alternatives to the whole range of dairy products. The most widely available include:

● Soy

This is the most commonly used replacement for dairy milk and comes in many forms. Made from pulverized soybeans, soy milk is interchangeable with cow's milk, being suitable for both cooking and drinking. Soy milk comes both chilled and in long-life cartons. It may be sweetened, unsweetened, fortified with extra calcium and vitamins, or flavored with chocolate, banana, or strawberry. Soy milk is also used to make cream, cheese, ice cream, and yogurt. Soy cheese is made from a blend of processed soybeans and vegetable oils and may be flavored with herbs and spices. There are also soy alternatives to Parmesan, Gouda, Cheddar, and cream cheese. Other nondairy cheeses include a Parmesan-type made from rice and another made from nuts and flavored with spices.

Tofu is also made from soybeans and has little flavor of its own but readily absorbs other stronger flavors, making it extremely versatile. Firm tofu comes in a block and can be marinated, roasted, stewed, or stir-fried. It is also available in a smoked form. Silken tofu has a softer texture and is used as

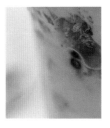
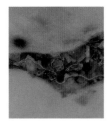

Watch out for ...

Sources of dairy products are not always easy to spot on food labels. If you notice any of the following, it is wise to check with the manufacturer: casein, hydrolysed casein, caseinate, albumen or albumin (may be sourced from eggs), lactic acid (E270), lactose, whey, nonfat milk solids, lacalbumin, nonfat milk powder, lactoglobulin, and monosodium glutamate (MSG).

Also avoid ...

Cow's, goat, and sheep's milk, butter, sour cream, buttermilk, smetana, cream, fromage frais, yogurt, crème fraîche, and ice cream.

Be aware ...

That the following may include dairy products: ready-prepared meals and desserts, pizza bases, sausages, pies, burgers, sauces, soups, ghee in Indian dishes (which may be clarified butter rather than being vegetable oil-based), wine, margarine, bouillon granules and cubes, cookies, cakes, pâté, dips, chocolate, and pastries.

an alternative to dairy cream or milk in desserts, sauces, dressings, and soups. Other forms of tofu, which are now readily available, include smoked, marinated, and deep fried. The latter is fairly tasteless but has an interesting texture and readily absorbs stronger flavors. Soy is a valuable source of calcium, iron, magnesium, phosphorus, and vitamin E.

● Rice

Rice milk avoids the slightly "floury" texture of soy milk and comes sweetened, unsweetened, and fortified with calcium. It is easily digested and almost nonallergenic.

● Nut

Crushed and ground almonds or cashews are mixed with water to make a versatile, mild-tasting milk. You can make your own by grinding nuts to a fine powder and blending with water. Add a banana and you have a delicious smoothie.

Breakfasts & Brunches

Numerous studies show that breakfast is an essential way to start the day, refueling the body and providing much-needed sustained energy. For those avoiding gluten, wheat, and dairy foods, breakfast need not be limited, as the following recipes demonstrate. There's a healthy apple granola, which can be made in advance, a creamy smoothie for when time is short, as well as more substantial cooked brunches that are perfect for leisurely weekends.

serves 4

Berry & Yogurt Crunch

Ingredients

generous ³/₄ cup rice, buckwheat, or millet flakes, or a mixture

4 tbsp honey

1 lb 2 oz/500 g thick plain soy yogurt or dairy-free alternative

finely grated rind of 1 orange

1 cup frozen mixed berries, partially thawed, plus extra to decorate

Nutritional Fact

Choose a yogurt with added "beneficial bacteria" such as acidophilus or bifidobacteria—they can help to heal the gut and address food intolerances.

Serving Analysis

* Calories 198
* Protein 6g
* Carbohydrate 39g
* Sugars 22g
* Fat 3.5g
* Saturates 0.5g

1 Heat a dry skillet over medium heat, add the flakes, and toast, shaking the skillet, for 1 minute. Add half the honey and stir to coat the flakes. Cook, stirring constantly, until the flakes turn golden brown and slightly crisp.

2 Put the yogurt into a bowl and stir in the remaining honey and the orange rind. Gently stir in the berries, reserving a few to decorate. Let stand for 10–15 minutes for the berries to release their juices, then stir again to give a swirl of color.

3 To serve, spoon a layer of flakes into the bottom of 4 glasses, then top with a layer of the berry yogurt. Sprinkle with another layer of flakes and add another layer of the yogurt. Decorate with the reserved berries.

serves 4

Buckwheat Crêpes with Maple Syrup Bananas

Ingredients

generous ¹/₃ cup buckwheat flour

generous ¹/₃ cup gluten-free all-purpose flour

pinch of salt

I large egg, lightly beaten

¹/₂ cup dairy-free milk

¹/₂ cup water

3 tbsp dairy-free margarine

For the maple syrup bananas

3 tbsp dairy-free margarine

2 tbsp maple syrup

2 bananas, thickly sliced diagonally

I Sift both types of flour and the salt into a mixing bowl. Make a well in the center and add the beaten egg, milk, and water. Using a balloon whisk, gradually mix the flour into the liquid ingredients, whisking well to get rid of any lumps, until you have a smooth batter.

2 Melt 2 tablespoons of the margarine in a small pan and stir it into the batter. Pour the batter into a pitcher, cover, and let rest for 30 minutes.

3 Melt half the remaining margarine in a medium-size skillet. When the skillet is hot, pour in enough batter to make a thin crêpe, swirling the skillet to make an even layer.

4 Cook one side until lightly browned, then, using a spatula, turn over and cook the other side. Slide onto a warm plate and cover with foil while you cook the remaining crêpes, adding more margarine when needed.

5 To make the maple syrup bananas, wipe the skillet, add the margarine, and heat until melted. Stir in the maple syrup, then add the bananas and cook for 2–3 minutes, or until the bananas have just softened and the sauce has thickened and caramelized. To serve, fold the crêpes in half and then half again, then top with bananas.

Nutritional Fact
Unusually for a plant-based food, buckwheat is a complete protein, containing all the essential amino acids. It also lowers blood cholesterol.

Serving Analysis

- *Calories*   339
- *Protein*   5.5g
- *Carbohydrate*   40g
- *Sugars*   13.5g
- *Fat*   19g
- *Saturates*   3.75g

serves 4

Millet Porridge with Apricot Purée

Ingredients

1 1/3 cups millet flakes

2 cups dairy-free milk

pinch of salt

freshly grated nutmeg

For the apricot purée

2/3 cup no-soak dried apricots, coarsely chopped

1 1/4 cups water

Nutritional Fact
Millet is high in protein and is a rich source of B vitamins that you may miss when cutting out grains containing gluten.

Serving Analysis
- *Calories* — 280
- *Protein* — 10g
- *Carbohydrate* — 49.5g
- *Sugars* — 16.g
- *Fat* — 4.75g
- *Saturates* — 0.7g

1 To make the apricot purée, put the apricots into a pan and cover with the water. Bring to a boil, then reduce the heat and let simmer, half covered, for 20 minutes until the apricots are very tender. Transfer the apricots, along with any water left in the pan, to a food processor or blender and process until smooth. Set aside.

2 To make the porridge, put the millet flakes into a pan and add the milk and salt. Bring to a boil, then reduce the heat and let simmer for 5 minutes, stirring frequently, until cooked and creamy. To serve, spoon into 4 bowls and top with the apricot purée and a little nutmeg.

makes 10 portions

Apple Granola

Ingredients

generous $^1/_3$ cup sunflower seeds

scant $^1/_4$ cup pepitas

scant $^5/_8$ cup shelled hazelnuts, coarsely chopped

generous $1^1/_4$ cups buckwheat flakes

generous $1^1/_4$ cups rice flakes

$^3/_4$ cup millet flakes

$^2/_3$ cup no-soak dried apple, coarsely chopped

$^2/_3$ cup dried pitted dates, coarsely chopped

Nutritional Fact
Sunflower seeds and pepitas contain essential omega oils that are vital for the health of the gut, skin, and immune system.

Serving Analysis

• Calories	340
• Protein	8.7g
• Carbohydrate	48g
• Sugars	15g
• Fat	15g
• Saturates	1.75g

1 Heat a dry skillet over medium heat, add the seeds and hazelnuts, and lightly toast, shaking the skillet frequently, for 4 minutes, or until golden brown. Transfer to a large mixing bowl and let cool.

2 Add the flakes, apple, and dates to the bowl and mix thoroughly until combined. Store the granola in an airtight jar or container.

serves 3–4

Almond & Banana Smoothie

Ingredients

scant 1 cup whole blanched almonds

2¹/₂ cups dairy-free milk

2 ripe bananas, halved

1 tsp natural vanilla extract

ground cinnamon, for sprinkling

1 Put the almonds into a food processor and process until very finely chopped. Add the milk, bananas, and vanilla extract and blend until smooth and creamy. Pour into glasses and sprinkle with cinnamon.

Nutritional Fact
Almonds help to reduce cravings that often form part of an intolerance. They also help to reduce cholesterol.

Serving Analysis

• Calories	282
• Protein	10.4g
• Carbohydrate	22g
• Sugars	12.5g
• Fat	19g
• Saturates	1.9g

serves 3–4

Sausage & Potato Brunch

Ingredients

4 gluten-free sausages or vegetarian alternative

corn oil, for cooking

4 boiled potatoes, cooled and diced

8 cherry tomatoes

4 eggs, beaten

salt and pepper

Nutritional Fact
Eggs are an excellent breakfast food as they contain sulfur, which helps the liver clear out waste products and toxins.

Serving Analysis
- Calories   435
- Protein   17g
- Carbohydrate   22g
- Sugars   2.5g
- Fat   30g
- Saturates   10.7g

1 Preheat the broiler to medium-high. Arrange the sausages on a foil-lined broiler pan and cook under the preheated broiler, turning occasionally, for 12–15 minutes, or until cooked through and golden brown. Let cool slightly, then slice into bite-size pieces.

2 Meanwhile, heat a little oil in a medium-size (10-inch/25-cm), heavy-bottom skillet with a heatproof handle over medium heat. Add the potatoes and cook until golden brown and crisp all over, then add the tomatoes and cook for an additional 2 minutes. Arrange the sausages in the skillet so that there is an even distribution of potatoes, tomatoes, and sausages.

3 Add a little more oil to the skillet if it seems dry. Season the beaten eggs to taste and pour the mixture over the ingredients in the skillet. Cook for 3 minutes, without stirring or disturbing the eggs. Place the skillet under the preheated broiler for 3 minutes, or until the top is just cooked. Cut into wedges to serve.

serves 4

Potato Cakes with Bacon & Maple Syrup

Ingredients

4 oz/115 g cold mashed potatoes

scant 1 cup dairy-free milk

$^1/_2$ cup gluten-free self-rising flour

pinch of salt

1 egg, beaten

corn oil, for cooking

To serve

8 good-quality bacon slices, broiled until crisp

1$^1/_2$ tbsp maple syrup

Nutritional Fact

Starting the day with a hearty and substantial breakfast can help to ensure sustained energy release throughout the morning.

Serving Analysis

• Calories	217
• Protein	8.1g
• Carbohydrate	28g
• Sugars	5.3g
• Fat	9.3g
• Saturates	2.5g

1 Put the mashed potatoes and milk into a food processor or blender and process to a thin purée.

2 Sift the flour and salt into a mixing bowl, make a well in the center of the flour, and add the beaten egg and potato purée. Using a balloon whisk, gradually mix the flour into the liquid ingredients, whisking well to make a smooth, creamy, fairly thick batter.

3 Heat a little oil in a large, nonstick skillet. Pour a small ladleful of batter per cake into the skillet—you will probably fit about 3 in the skillet at one time. Cook each cake for 2 minutes on each side until golden brown. Remove from the skillet and keep warm while you cook the remaining potato cakes.

4 Divide the cakes between 4 warmed plates, top each serving with 2 bacon slices, and drizzle with maple syrup.

Soups & Light Meals

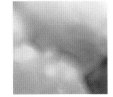

Warming, healthy, and filling, the soups in this chapter
are simple to prepare and make use of readily available
ingredients. They can also be made in advance, making them
perfect for families who eat at varying times, enabling
everyone to enjoy the same nutritious meal. The recipes cater
for all eating occasions from the quick snack to the light
summery lunch but can also be turned into more substantial
meals when combined with other recipes in this book.

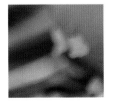

serves 4

Spicy Carrot & Lentil Soup

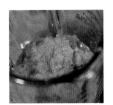

Ingredients

2 tbsp olive oil

1 large onion, chopped

1 celery stalk, chopped

1 potato, diced

6 carrots, sliced

1 tsp paprika

2 tsp ground cumin

1 tsp ground coriander

$^1/_2$ tsp chili powder (optional)

scant 1 cup red split lentils

5 cups vegetable or
chicken stock

2 bay leaves

salt and pepper

2 tbsp chopped fresh cilantro,
to garnish

Nutritional Fact

*Traditionally used to
treat flatulence, cumin
is known to aid
digestion and improve
circulation to the
gastrointestinal tract.*

Serving Analysis

• *Calories*   277

• *Protein*   13g

• *Carbohydrate*   40g

• *Sugars*   7g

• *Fat*   8.5g

• *Saturates*   0.25g

1 Heat the oil in a large, heavy-bottom pan over medium-low heat. Add the onion and cook for 7 minutes, stirring occasionally. Add the celery, potato, and carrots and cook for an additional 5 minutes, stirring occasionally. Stir in the paprika, cumin, ground coriander, and chili powder, if using, and cook for an additional minute.

2 Stir in the lentils, stock, and bay leaves. Bring to a boil, then reduce the heat and let simmer, half-covered, over low heat, stirring occasionally to prevent the lentils sticking to the bottom of the pan, for 25 minutes, or until the lentils are tender.

3 Remove and discard the bay leaves. Transfer to a food processor or blender, or use a hand blender, and process the soup until thick and smooth. Return to the pan and reheat. Season to taste with salt and pepper and add extra chili powder, if liked. Ladle into 4 warmed bowls and sprinkle with fresh cilantro before serving.

serves 4

Roasted Onion Soup with Cornmeal Croutons

Ingredients

1 lb 12 oz/800 g red onions, peeled and quartered

1 tbsp olive oil

1 tbsp dairy-free margarine

salt and pepper

scant 1 1/4 cups dry white wine

5 cups vegetable stock

1 fresh rosemary sprig, plus extra to garnish

1 tsp chopped fresh thyme

1 tsp Dijon mustard

For the croutons

1 1/4 cups water

generous 3/8 cup fine instant cornmeal

1/2 tsp salt

1 tbsp chopped fresh rosemary

olive oil, for brushing

1 Preheat the oven to 400°F/200°C. Put the onions and oil into a roasting pan and toss well. Dot with the margarine, season to taste with salt, and roast in the preheated oven for 45 minutes, turning occasionally, until very tender and slightly blackened around the edges. Remove from the oven and let cool slightly.

2 Discard the outer layer of each onion segment if crisp, then cut the remainder into thick slices. Put the onions into a large, heavy-bottom pan with the wine and bring to a boil. Cook until most of the wine has evaporated and the smell of alcohol has disappeared.

3 Stir in the stock and herbs and cook over medium-low heat for 30–35 minutes, or until reduced and thickened. Stir in the mustard and season to taste with salt and pepper.

4 Meanwhile, to make the cornmeal croutons, heat the water to boiling point in a pan. Pour in the cornmeal in a steady stream and cook, stirring constantly with a wooden spoon, for 5 minutes, or until thickened and the mixture starts to come away from the sides of the pan. Stir in the salt and rosemary.

5 Cover a cutting board with a sheet of plastic wrap, then, using a spatula, spread out the cornmeal in an even layer about 1/2 inch/1 cm thick. Let cool and firm up. Cut into bite-size cubes, brush with oil, and arrange on a baking sheet. Cook in the oven, turning occasionally, for 10–15 minutes, or until crisp and lightly golden brown.

6 Remove and discard the rosemary from the soup. Transfer half the soup to a food processor or blender and process until smooth, then return to the pan and stir well. To serve, ladle into 4 warmed bowls, and top with the cornmeal croutons and sprigs of rosemary.

Nutritional Fact

Onions contain sulfur, which is a very important component of all body tissues, and may help to heal the gut, as well as protect against cancer.

Serving Analysis

- Calories 218
- Protein 3.2g
- Carbohydrate 22.5g
- Sugars 8.7g
- Fat 8.7g
- Saturates 0.6g

serves 4–6

Herby Potato Salad

Ingredients

1 lb 2 oz/500 g new potatoes

salt and pepper

16 vine-ripened cherry tomatoes, halved

generous $^3/_8$ cup black olives, pitted and coarsely chopped

4 scallions, finely sliced

2 tbsp chopped fresh mint

2 tbsp chopped fresh parsley

2 tbsp chopped fresh cilantro

juice of 1 lemon

3 tbsp extra virgin olive oil

1 Cook the potatoes in a pan of lightly salted boiling water for 15 minutes, or until tender. Drain, then let cool slightly before peeling off the skins. Cut into halves or quarters, depending on the size of the potato. Then combine with the tomatoes, olives, scallions, and herbs in a salad bowl.

2 Mix the lemon juice and oil together in a small bowl or pitcher and pour over the potato salad. Season to taste with salt and pepper before serving.

Nutritional Fact

Parsley can help ease food intolerances by assisting the adrenal glands. Overworked adrenals mean that energy and nutrients that could help deal with intolerances are diverted from the gut.

Serving Analysis
- *Calories*   202
- *Protein*   2.5g
- *Carbohydrate*   25.5g
- *Sugars*   2.8g
- *Fat*   11.2g
- *Saturates*   0.06g

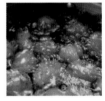

serves 4

Tabbouleh

Ingredients

generous 1 cup quinoa

2¹/₂ cups water

10 vine-ripened cherry tomatoes, seeded and chopped

3-inch/7.5-cm piece cucumber, diced

3 scallions, finely chopped

juice of ¹/₂ lemon

2 tbsp extra virgin olive oil

4 tbsp chopped fresh mint

4 tbsp chopped fresh cilantro

4 tbsp chopped fresh parsley

salt and pepper

Nutritional Fact

The super-nutritious grain quinoa is used here instead of the usual bulgur wheat or couscous to make this filling salad. It is at its most flavorful when served at room temperature.

Serving Analysis

• *Calories*	*283*
• *Protein*	*8.3g*
• *Carbohydrate*	*43g*
• *Sugars*	*6.8g*
• *Fat*	*10.4g*
• *Saturates*	*0.38g*

1 Put the quinoa into a medium-size pan and cover with the water. Bring to a boil, then reduce the heat, cover, and let simmer over low heat for 15 minutes. Drain if necessary.

2 Let the quinoa cool slightly before combining with the remaining ingredients in a salad bowl. Season to taste with salt and pepper before serving.

serves 4

Walnut, Pear & Crispy Bacon Salad

Ingredients

4 lean bacon slices

generous ⁵/₈ cup walnut halves

2 Red Bartlett pears, cored and sliced lengthwise

1 tbsp lemon juice

6 oz/175 g watercress, tough stalks removed

For the dressing

3 tbsp extra virgin olive oil

2 tbsp lemon juice

¹/₂ tsp honey

salt and pepper

Nutritional Fact
Watercress contains good levels of beta-carotene and lutein, plant chemicals that give it its color and help to support the immune system.

Serving Analysis
* Calories   433
* Protein   6.3g
* Carbohydrate   18g
* Sugars   11.8g
* Fat   39.5g
* Saturates   1g

1 Preheat the broiler to high. Arrange the bacon on a foil-lined broiler pan and cook under the preheated broiler until well browned and crisp. Let cool, then cut into ¹/₂-inch/1-cm pieces.

2 Meanwhile, heat a dry skillet over medium heat and lightly toast the walnuts, shaking the skillet frequently, for 3 minutes, or until lightly browned. Let cool.

3 Toss the pears in the lemon juice to prevent discoloration. Put the watercress, walnuts, pears, and bacon into a salad bowl.

4 To make the dressing, whisk the oil, lemon juice, and honey together in a small bowl or pitcher. Season to taste with salt and pepper, then pour over the salad. Toss well to combine and serve.

serves 2 as a main course or 4 as an appetizer

Buckwheat Noodle Salad with Smoked Tofu

Ingredients

7 oz/200 g buckwheat noodles

9 oz/250 g firm smoked tofu (drained weight)

7 oz/200 g white cabbage, finely shredded

9 oz/250 g carrots, finely shredded

3 scallions, diagonally sliced

1 fresh red chili, seeded and finely sliced into circles

2 tbsp sesame seeds, lightly toasted

For the dressing

1 tsp grated fresh gingerroot

1 garlic clove, crushed

6 oz/175 g silken tofu (drained weight)

4 tsp tamari (wheat-free soy sauce)

2 tbsp sesame oil

4 tbsp hot water

salt

Nutritional Fact
Cabbage is a member of the brassica family, along with broccoli, cauliflower, kale, and Brussels sprouts, which all aid liver function.

Serving Analysis

• Calories	326
• Protein	16g
• Carbohydrate	50g
• Sugars	4g
• Fat	9g
• Saturates	1g

1 Cook the noodles in a large pan of lightly salted boiling water according to the package instructions. Drain and refresh under cold running water.

2 To make the dressing, blend the ginger, garlic, silken tofu, soy sauce, oil, and water together in a small bowl until smooth and creamy. Season to taste with salt.

3 Place the smoked tofu in a steamer. Steam for 5 minutes, then cut into thin slices.

4 Meanwhile, put the cabbage, carrots, scallions, and chili into a bowl and toss to mix. To serve, arrange the noodles on serving plates and top with the carrot salad and slices of tofu. Spoon over the dressing and sprinkle with sesame seeds.

serves 4–6

Baba Ghanoush with Flat Breads

Ingredients

1 large eggplant, pricked all over with a fork

3 fat garlic cloves, unpeeled

1 tsp ground coriander

1 tsp ground cumin

1 tbsp light sesame seed paste

juice of $1/2$ lemon

2 tbsp extra virgin olive oil

salt and pepper

fresh cilantro, to garnish

For the flat breads

scant 2 cups gluten-free white bread flour

2 tbsp fine cornmeal

1 tsp gluten-free baking powder

1 tsp salt

scant 4 tbsp dairy-free margarine, diced

1 tbsp sesame seeds (optional)

$2/3$–$3/4$ cup warm water

corn oil, for oiling

1 To make the baba ghanoush, preheat the oven to 400°F/200°C. Put the eggplant into a roasting pan and bake in the preheated oven for 25 minutes. Add the garlic cloves to the pan and cook for an additional 15 minutes until the eggplant and garlic are very tender.

2 Halve the eggplant and scoop out the flesh with a spoon into a food processor or blender. Peel the garlic cloves and add to the food processor or blender with the spices, sesame seed paste, lemon juice, and oil. Process until smooth and creamy, then season to taste with salt and pepper. Transfer to a serving dish and cover until required.

3 Meanwhile, make the flat breads. Sift the flour, cornmeal, baking powder, and salt into a mixing bowl, then rub in the margarine with your fingertips until the mixture resembles bread crumbs. Add the sesame seeds, if using, and stir in the water, first with a wooden spoon, then with your hands to bring the mixture together into a ball, adding more water or flour as necessary.

4 Turn the mixture out onto a lightly floured counter and knead lightly until a soft dough forms. Divide into 6 pieces, then roll each piece into a ball. Wrap in plastic wrap and let rest in the refrigerator for 30 minutes.

5 Roll out or press the dough balls with your fingers into $1/4$-inch/5-mm thick circles—it is quite crumbly and fragile, so don't worry if the edges are slightly rough. Heat a lightly oiled grill pan over medium heat and cook each flat bread for a few minutes on each side until lightly golden, keeping them warm while you finish cooking the remainder. Serve warm with the baba ghanoush.

Nutritional Fact

Garlic is a potent natural antibiotic, which can help to keep the gut clear of the microbes that can contribute to digestive problems.

Serving Analysis

- Calories   377
- Protein   6g
- Carbohydrate   51g
- Sugars   3.2g
- Fat   18g
- Saturates   2g

makes 16 rolls

Vietnamese Rolls with Caramelized Pork & Noodles

Ingredients

2 tbsp tamari (wheat-free soy sauce)

1 1/2 tsp maple syrup

1 lb 2 oz/500 g lean pork loin

vegetable oil, for cooking

32 rice paper wrappers

2 1/2 oz/70 g rice vermicelli noodles, cooked

To serve

gluten-free hoisin sauce

strips of cucumber

strips of scallion

Nutritional Fact

Fermented soy (found in tamari) is good for liver function. When our hormones are out of balance, the liver has to work hard processing these extra hormones. Since soy can help to balance hormones, the liver has a lighter load.

Serving Analysis

• Calories	109
• Protein	7g
• Carbohydrate	8g
• Sugars	0.7g
• Fat	5g
• Saturates	0.08g

1 Blend the tamari and maple syrup together in a shallow dish. Add the pork and turn to coat in the mixture. Cover and let marinate in the refrigerator for at least 1 hour or preferably overnight.

2 Heat a grill pan over medium-high heat until hot, add a little oil to cover the bottom, and cook the pork for 4–6 minutes each side, depending on the thickness of the loin, until cooked and caramelized on the outside. Remove from the pan and slice into fine strips.

3 Fill a heatproof bowl with water that is just off the boil. Put 2 rice paper wrappers on top of one another (you will need 2 per roll as they are very thin and fragile) and soak in the water for 20 seconds, or until they turn pliable and opaque. Carefully remove using a spatula, drain for a second, and place flat on a plate.

4 Spread a spoonful of hoisin sauce over the wrapper and top with a small bundle of noodles and a few strips of pork, cucumber, and scallion. Fold in the ends and sides of the wrapper to resemble an egg roll. Set aside while you make the remaining rolls. Slice in half on the diagonal and serve with a little more hoisin sauce, if liked.

serves 2 as a main course or 4 as an appetizer

Mixed Sushi Rolls

1 Put the rice into a pan and cover with cold water. Bring to a boil, then reduce the heat, cover, and let simmer for 15–20 minutes, or until the rice is tender and the water has been absorbed. Drain if necessary and transfer to a bowl. Mix the vinegar, sugar and salt together, then, using a spatula, stir well into the rice. Cover with a damp cloth and let cool.

2 To make the rolls, lay a clean bamboo mat over a cutting board. Lay a sheet of nori, shiny side-down, on the mat. Spread a quarter of the rice mixture over the nori, using wet fingers to press it down evenly, leaving a $^1/_2$-inch/1-cm margin at the top and bottom.

3 For smoked salmon and cucumber rolls, lay the salmon over the rice and arrange the cucumber in a line across the center. For the shrimp rolls, lay the shrimp and avocado in a line across the center.

4 Carefully hold the nearest edge of the mat, then, using the mat as a guide, roll up the nori tightly to make a neat tube of rice enclosing the filling. Seal the uncovered edge with a little water, then roll the sushi off the mat. Repeat to make 3 more rolls—you need 2 salmon and cucumber and 2 shrimp and avocado in total.

5 Using a wet knife, cut each roll into 8 pieces and stand upright on a platter. Wipe and rinse the knife between cuts to prevent the rice sticking. Serve the rolls with wasabi, tamari, and pickled ginger.

Ingredients

4 sheets nori (seaweed) for rolling

For the rice

scant 1 $^1/_4$ cups sushi rice

2 tbsp rice vinegar

1 tsp superfine sugar

$^1/_2$ tsp salt

For the fillings

1 $^3/_4$ oz/50 g smoked salmon

1 $^1/_2$-inch/4-cm piece cucumber, peeled, seeded, and cut into short thin sticks

1 $^1/_2$ oz/40 g cooked shelled shrimp

1 small avocado, pitted, peeled, thinly sliced, and tossed in lemon juice

To serve

wasabi (Japanese horseradish sauce)

tamari (wheat-free soy sauce)

pink pickled ginger

Nutritional Fact
Nori is the seaweed with the most amount of protein. It also helps to rid the body of toxic metals.

Serving Analysis

• Calories	195
• Protein	7.5g
• Carbohydrate	23g
• Sugars	3.6g
• Fat	8.4g
• Saturates	1.4g

Seafood, Meat & Poultry

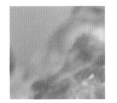  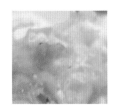  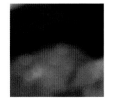 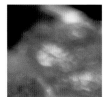

Inspired by a cross-section of cultures and flavors, this chapter features fragrant Malaysian-style coconut noodles with shrimp, Italian pasta with a meat ball sauce, and a creamy southern Indian chicken curry, while traveling closer to home, there's a hearty beef stew with herby dumplings—all without a trace of gluten, wheat, or dairy.

  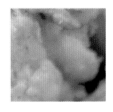 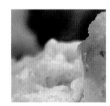  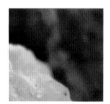

serves 4–6

Smoked Haddock & Shrimp Tart

Ingredients

14 oz/400 g undyed smoked haddock or cod fillet, rinsed and dried

1 1/4 cups dairy-free milk

5 1/2 oz/150 g cooked shelled shrimp

7/8 cup vegan cream cheese

3 eggs, beaten

3 tbsp snipped fresh chives

pepper

For the pie dough

generous 1 3/8 cups gluten-free all-purpose flour

large pinch of salt

3 1/2 oz/100 g dairy-free margarine, diced, plus extra for greasing

1 egg yolk

3 tbsp ice-cold water

1 Preheat the oven to 400°F/200°C. Lightly grease a 10 1/2-inch/26-cm tart dish.

2 To make the pie dough, sift the flour and salt into a mixing bowl, then rub in the margarine with your fingertips until the mixture resembles coarse bread crumbs. Stir in the egg yolk, followed by the water, then bring the mixture together into a ball. Turn out onto a lightly floured counter and knead until smooth. Wrap in plastic wrap and let chill in the refrigerator for 30 minutes.

3 Meanwhile, put the fish into a shallow pan with the milk. Heat gently until simmering and let simmer for 10 minutes, or until just cooked and opaque. Remove the fish with a slotted spoon, let cool a little, then peel away the skin and discard any bones. Flake the fish into large chunks and set aside. Set aside 1/2 cup of the cooking liquid.

4 Roll out the dough and use to line the prepared tart dish. Line the pastry shell with parchment paper and dried beans and bake in the preheated oven for 8 minutes. Remove the paper and beans and bake for an additional 5 minutes.

5 Arrange the fish and shrimp in the pastry shell. Beat together the cream cheese, reserved cooking liquid, eggs, chives, and pepper to taste in a bowl, then pour over the seafood. Bake for 30 minutes, or until the filling is set and golden brown.

Nutritional Fact
Haddock and cod contain good amounts of vitamin A, which helps to heal the gut lining, a very important part of addressing food intolerances.

Serving Analysis

• Calories	592
• Protein	34g
• Carbohydrate	34g
• Sugars	1g
• Fat	35.5g
• Saturates	8.7g

serves 4

Baked Lemon Cod with Herb Sauce

Ingredients

4 thick cod fillets

olive oil, for brushing

8 thin lemon slices

salt and pepper

For the herb sauce

4 tbsp olive oil

1 garlic clove, crushed

4 tbsp chopped fresh parsley

2 tbsp chopped fresh mint

juice of ¹/₂ lemon

salt and pepper

Nutritional Fact
Olive oil remains relatively stable when heated and is therefore good for cooking. It has been shown to reduce cholesterol levels.

Serving Analysis
- *Calories*   *232*
- *Protein*   *21g*
- *Carbohydrate*   *2g*
- *Sugars*   *0.2g*
- *Fat*   *16g*
- *Saturates*   *0.1g*

1 Preheat the oven to 400°F/200°C. Rinse each cod fillet and pat dry with paper towels, then brush with oil. Place each fillet on a piece of parchment paper that is large enough to encase the fish in a package. Top each fillet with 2 lemon slices and season to taste with salt and pepper. Fold over the parchment paper to encase the fish and bake in the preheated oven for 20 minutes, or until just cooked and opaque.

2 Meanwhile, to make the herb sauce, put all the ingredients into a food processor and process until finely chopped. Season to taste with salt and pepper.

3 Carefully unfold each package and place on serving plates. Pour a spoonful of herb sauce over each piece of fish before serving.

serves 4

Malaysian-style Coconut Noodles with Shrimp

Ingredients

2 tbsp vegetable oil

I small red bell pepper, seeded and diced

7 oz/200 g bok choy, stalks thinly sliced and leaves chopped

2 large garlic cloves, chopped

I tsp ground turmeric

2 tsp garam masala

I tsp chili powder (optional)

$^1/_2$ cup hot vegetable stock

2 heaping tbsp smooth peanut butter

I $^1/_2$ cups coconut milk

I tbsp tamari (wheat-free soy sauce)

9 oz/250 g thick rice noodles

10 oz/280 g cooked shelled jumbo shrimp

 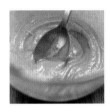 

To garnish

2 scallions, finely shredded

I tbsp sesame seeds

Nutritional Fact

Like mother's milk, coconut milk contains lauric acid, which protects against viruses and bacterial infections.

Serving Analysis

- *Calories*   428
- *Protein*   20g
- *Carbohydrate*   31g
- *Sugars*   10g
- *Fat*   26g
- *Saturates*   7g

I Heat the oil in a preheated wok or large, heavy-bottom skillet over high heat. Add the red bell pepper, bok choy stalks, and garlic and stir-fry for 3 minutes. Add the turmeric, garam masala, chili powder, if using, and bok choy leaves, and stir-fry for an additional minute.

2 Mix the hot stock and peanut butter together in a heatproof bowl until the peanut butter has dissolved, then add to the stir-fry with the coconut milk and tamari. Cook for 5 minutes over medium heat, or until reduced and thickened.

3 Meanwhile, immerse the noodles in a bowl of just boiled water. Let stand for 4 minutes, then drain and refresh the noodles under cold running water. Add the cooked noodles and shrimp to the coconut curry and cook for an additional 2–3 minutes, stirring frequently, until heated through.

4 Serve the noodle dish sprinkled with scallions and sesame seeds.

serves 2–3

Salmon Fingers with Potato Wedges

Ingredients

scant 1 cup fine cornmeal

1 tsp paprika

14 oz/400 g salmon fillet, skinned and sliced into 12 chunky fingers

1 egg, beaten

corn oil, for cooking

salt and pepper

For the potato wedges

1 lb 2 oz/500 g potatoes, scrubbed and cut into thick wedges

1–2 tbsp olive oil

1/2 tsp paprika

salt

Nutritional Fact
Salmon is an oily fish, high in omega-3 fatty acids, which help to protect the brain, eyes, heart, and liver.

Serving Analysis
- Calories   665
- Protein   35g
- Carbohydrate   73g
- Sugars   2g
- Fat   27g
- Saturates   4g

1 Preheat the oven to 400°F/200°C. To make the potato wedges, dry the potatoes on a clean dish towel. Spoon the oil into a roasting pan and put into the preheated oven briefly to heat. Toss the potatoes in the warm oil until well coated. Sprinkle with paprika and salt to taste and roast for 30 minutes, turning halfway through, until crisp and golden.

2 Meanwhile, mix the cornmeal and paprika together on a plate. Dip each salmon finger into the beaten egg, then roll in the cornmeal mixture until evenly coated.

3 Heat enough oil to cover the bottom of a large, heavy-bottom skillet over medium heat. Carefully arrange half the salmon fingers in the skillet and cook for 6 minutes, turning halfway through, until golden. Drain on paper towels and keep warm while you cook the remaining fingers. Serve with the potato wedges.

Nutritional Fact
Beef is a great source of iron, which is much more readily absorbed in the form found in meat rather than in plant sources.

Serving Analysis
- *Calories*   819
- *Protein*   38g
- *Carbohydrate*   35.5g
- *Sugars*   3.3g
- *Fat*   58g
- *Saturates*   20.4g

serves 4

Winter Beef Stew with Herb Dumplings

Ingredients

3 tbsp gluten-free all-purpose flour

salt and pepper

1 lb 12 oz/800 g rump steak, cubed

3 tbsp olive oil

12 shallots, peeled and halved, or quartered if large

2 carrots, cut into thin sticks

1 parsnip, sliced into circles

2 bay leaves

1 tbsp chopped fresh rosemary

2 cups cider

scant 1 1/4 cup beef stock

1 tbsp tamari (wheat-free soy sauce)

7 oz/200 g canned chestnuts, drained

For the herb dumplings

scant 1 cup gluten-free self-rising flour, plus extra for flouring

1 3/4 oz/50 g gluten-free vegetable suet

2 tbsp chopped fresh thyme

salt and pepper

1 Preheat the oven to 325°F/160°C. Put the flour into a clean plastic bag or on a plate and season generously with salt and pepper. Toss the beef in the seasoned flour until coated.

2 Heat 1 tablespoon of the oil in a large, ovenproof casserole dish over medium-high heat. Add one-third of the beef and cook for 5–6 minutes, turning occasionally, until browned all over—the meat may stick to the casserole until it is properly sealed. Remove the beef with a slotted spoon. Cook the remaining 2 batches, adding another tablespoon of oil as necessary. Set aside when all the beef has been sealed.

3 Add the remaining oil to the casserole with the shallots, carrots, parsnip, and herbs and cook for 3 minutes, stirring occasionally. Pour in the cider and beef stock and bring to a boil. Cook over high heat until the alcohol has evaporated and the liquid reduced. Add the stock and tamari, then cook for an additional 3 minutes.

4 Stir in the chestnuts and beef, cover, and cook in the preheated oven for 1 hour 35 minutes.

5 Meanwhile, to make the dumplings, combine all the ingredients in a bowl and season to taste with salt and pepper. Mix in enough water to make a soft dough. Divide the dough into walnut-size pieces and, using floured hands, roll each piece into a ball.

6 Add to the casserole dish, cover, and cook for an additional 25 minutes, or until the dumplings are cooked, the stock has formed a thick, rich gravy, and the meat is tender. Season to taste with salt and pepper before serving.

serves 4

Pasta with Italian Meat Ball Sauce

Ingredients

10¹/₂ oz/300 g dried gluten-free spaghetti

salt and pepper

For the meat balls

³/₄ cup fresh gluten-free bread crumbs

1 lb/450 g fresh lean ground beef

1 onion, grated

1 large garlic clove, crushed

1 egg, beaten

salt and pepper

For the tomato sauce

1 tbsp olive oil

2 garlic cloves, chopped

2 tsp dried oregano

1¹/₄ cups dry white wine

2¹/₂ cups strained tomatoes

1 bay leaf

2 tsp tomato paste

¹/₂ tsp sugar

Nutritional Fact
Tomatoes are rich in an antioxidant called lycopene, which helps immune function and gut healing.

Serving Analysis

• Calories	732
• Protein	36g
• Carbohydrate	87g
• Sugars	10g
• Fat	21g
• Saturates	5.3g

1 To make the meat balls, put the bread crumbs, ground meat, onion, garlic, and egg into a bowl and mix well until combined. Season to taste with salt and pepper, cover, and let chill in the refrigerator for 30 minutes.

2 Meanwhile, make the tomato sauce. Heat the oil in a large, heavy-bottom skillet over medium heat and sauté the garlic, stirring, for 1 minute. Add the oregano and cook, stirring, for an additional minute. Pour in the wine and cook over high heat until it has almost evaporated.

3 Add the strained tomatoes, bay leaf, tomato paste, and sugar, then stir well. Partially cover the skillet and cook over medium-low heat for 5 minutes.

4 Form the meat ball mixture into walnut-size balls. Add to the sauce, partially cover, and cook for 15–20 minutes, or until the meat balls are cooked through.

5 Meanwhile, cook the pasta in a large pan of lightly salted boiling water according to the package instructions. Drain, reserving 3 tablespoons of the cooking liquid. Stir the cooking liquid into the sauce before serving with the pasta.

serves 4

Lamb Koftas with Chickpea Mash

Ingredients

1 1/8 cups fresh lean ground lamb

1 onion, finely chopped

1 tbsp chopped fresh coriander

1 tbsp chopped fresh parsley

1/2 tsp ground coriander

1/4 tsp chili powder

salt and pepper

For the chickpea mash

1 tbsp olive oil

2 garlic cloves, chopped

14 oz/400 g canned chickpeas, drained and rinsed

1/4 cup dairy-free milk

salt and pepper

2 tbsp chopped fresh cilantro

Nutritional Fact
Chickpeas, like all legumes, are high in soluble fiber, which helps to clean out the gut by absorbing and eliminating toxins via the bowel.

Serving Analysis
- *Calories*   349
- *Protein*   21g
- *Carbohydrate* 19g
- *Sugars*   1.7g
- *Fat*   21g
- *Saturates*   5.1g

1 Put the lamb, onion, herbs, spices, and salt and pepper to taste in a food processor. Process until thoroughly combined.

2 Divide the mixture into 8 portions and, using wet hands, shape each portion into a sausage shape around a wooden skewer (soaked in water first to prevent burning). Cover and chill the skewers in the refrigerator for 30 minutes.

3 To cook, preheat a grilling pan over a medium heat and brush with a little oil. Cook the skewers in 2 batches, turning occasionally, for 10 minutes, or until browned on all sides and cooked through.

4 To make the chickpea mash, heat the oil in a pan and gently sauté the garlic for 2 minutes. Add the chickpeas and milk and heat through for a few minutes. Transfer to a food processor or blender and process until smooth. Season to taste with salt and pepper, then stir in the fresh cilantro. Serve the mash with the koftas.

serves 4

Creamy Chicken Curry with Lemon Rice

Ingredients

2 tbsp vegetable oil

4 skinless, boneless chicken breasts, about 1 lb 12 oz/800 g in total, cut into 1-inch/2.5-cm pieces

1 1/2 tsp cumin seeds

1 large onion, grated

2 fresh green chilies, finely chopped

2 large garlic cloves, grated

1 tbsp grated fresh gingerroot

1 tsp ground turmeric

1 tsp ground coriander

1 tsp garam masala

1 1/4 cups coconut milk

9 fl oz/250 ml canned chopped tomatoes

2 tsp lemon juice

salt

2 tbsp chopped fresh cilantro, to garnish

 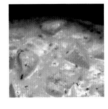 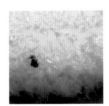

For the lemon rice

scant 1 3/4 cups basmati rice, rinsed

5 cups water

juice and grated rind of 1 lemon

3 cloves

1 Heat the oil in a large, heavy-bottom pan over medium heat. Add the chicken and cook for 5–8 minutes, turning frequently, until lightly browned and cooked through. Remove from the pan and set aside. Add the cumin seeds and cook until they start to darken and sizzle. Stir in the onion, partially cover, and cook over medium-low heat, stirring frequently, for 10 minutes, or until soft and golden. Add the chilies, garlic, ginger, turmeric, ground coriander, and garam masala and cook for 1 minute.

2 Return the chicken to the pan and stir in the coconut milk and tomatoes. Partially cover and cook over medium heat for 15 minutes until the sauce has reduced and thickened. Stir in the lemon juice and season to taste with salt.

3 Meanwhile, make the rice. Put the rice into a pan and cover with the water. Add the lemon juice and cloves. Bring to a boil, then reduce the heat, cover, and let simmer over very low heat for 15 minutes, or until the rice is tender and all the water has been absorbed. Remove the pan from the heat and stir in the lemon rind. Let the rice stand, covered, for 5 minutes.

4 Serve the curry with the lemon rice, sprinkled with fresh cilantro.

Nutritional Fact

A potent anti-inflammatory, ginger has been used for centuries to treat stomach upsets, nausea, heartburn, abdominal cramps, and travel sickness.

Serving Analysis

- Calories   545
- Protein   46g
- Carbohydrate   29g
- Sugars   5.9g
- Fat   27g
- Saturates   6.8g

serves 4

Roasted Chicken with Sun-Blush Tomato Pesto

Ingredients

4 skinless, boneless chicken breasts, about 1 lb 12 oz/800 g in total

1 tbsp olive oil

salt and pepper

For the Pesto

4^{1}/$_{2}$ oz/125 g sun-blush tomatoes in oil (drained weight), chopped

2 garlic cloves, crushed

6 tbsp pine nuts, lightly toasted

^{2}/$_{3}$ cup extra virgin olive oil

1 Preheat the oven to 400°F/200°C. To make the red pesto, put the sun-blush tomatoes, garlic, 4 tablespoons of the pine nuts, and oil into a food processor and process to a coarse paste.

2 Arrange the chicken in a large, ovenproof dish or roasting pan. Brush each breast with the oil, then place a tablespoon of red pesto over each breast. Using the back of a spoon, spread the pesto so that it covers the top of each breast. This pesto recipe makes more than just the 4 tablespoons used here. Store the extra pesto in an airtight container in the refrigerator for up to 1 week.

3 Roast the chicken in the preheated oven for 30 minutes, or until tender and the juices run clear when a skewer is inserted into the thickest part of the meat.

4 Serve sprinkled with the remaining toasted pine nuts.

Nutritional Fact

Pine nuts are nuts with a high protein content and also vitamin E, both of which help to repair structures in the gut.

Serving Analysis

• Calories	558
• Protein	21g
• Carbohydrate	9.5g
• Sugars	0.5g
• Fat	51g
• Saturates	2.1g

Vegetarian

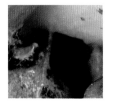

For those who avoid meat, poultry, or fish, or simply want to cut down on the amount they eat, this collection of appetizing and nourishing dishes is sure to inspire. The emphasis is on simple ingredients, including plenty of healthy vegetables, used in imaginative ways such as the North African eggplant tagine with cornmeal mash, Thai tofu cakes with a zingy sweet chili dip, along with a classic Spanish tortilla.

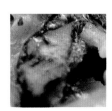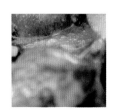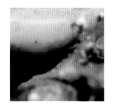

serves 4

Rösti with Roasted Vegetables

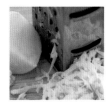

Ingredients

2 lb/900 g potatoes, halved if large

salt and pepper

corn oil, for cooking

For the vegan pesto dressing

2 tbsp vegan pesto

1 tbsp boiling water

1 tbsp extra virgin olive oil

For the roasted vegetables

2 tbsp extra virgin olive oil

1 tbsp balsamic vinegar

1 tsp honey

1 red bell pepper, seeded and quartered

2 zucchini, sliced lengthwise

2 red onions, quartered

1 small fennel bulb, cut into thin wedges

16 vine-ripened tomatoes

8 garlic cloves

2 fresh rosemary sprigs

1 For the roasted vegetables, mix the oil, vinegar, and honey together in a large, shallow dish. Add the red bell pepper, zucchini, onions, fennel, tomatoes, garlic, and rosemary to the dish and toss in the marinade. Let marinate for at least 1 hour.

2 Preheat the oven to 400°F/200°C. Cook the potatoes in a pan of lightly salted boiling water for 8–10 minutes, or until partially cooked. Let cool, then coarsely grate.

3 Transfer the vegetables, except the tomatoes and garlic, and the marinade to a roasting pan. Roast in the preheated oven for 25 minutes, then add the tomatoes and garlic and roast for an additional 15 minutes, or until the vegetables are tender and slightly blackened around the edges.

4 Meanwhile, cook the rösti. Take a quarter of the potato mixture in your hands and form into a roughly shaped cake. Heat just enough oil to cover the bottom of a skillet over medium heat. Put the cakes, 2 at a time, into the skillet and flatten with a spatula to form circles about ³/₄ inch/2 cm thick.

5 Cook the rösti for 6 minutes on each side, or until golden brown and crisp. Mix the dressing ingredients. To serve, top each rösti with the roasted vegetables and drizzle with a little pesto dressing. Season to taste.

Nutritional Fact

Rosemary contains fat-soluble antioxidants that reduce the free radicals produced when oil is heated.

Serving Analysis

• Calories	447
• Protein	9g
• Carbohydrate	74g
• Sugars	19g
• Fat	15.5g
• Saturates	1g

serves 4

Mixed Vegetable Curry with Chickpea Pancakes

Ingredients

7 oz/200 g carrots, cut into chunks
10¹/₂ oz/300 g potatoes, quartered
2 tbsp vegetable oil
1¹/₂ tsp cumin seeds
seeds from 5 green cardamom pods
1¹/₂ tsp mustard seeds
2 onions, grated
1 tsp ground turmeric
1 tsp ground coriander
1 bay leaf
1¹/₂ tsp chili powder
1 tbsp grated fresh gingerroot
2 large garlic cloves, crushed
scant 1¹/₄ cups strained tomatoes
scant 1 cup vegetable stock
1 cup frozen peas
generous ¹/₂ cup frozen spinach leaves
salt

For the chickpea pancakes

generous 1¹/₂ cups gram or chickpea flour
1 tsp salt
¹/₂ tsp baking soda
1³/₄ cups water
vegetable oil, for cooking

1 To make the pancakes, sift the flour, salt, and baking soda into a large mixing bowl. Make a well in the center and add the water. Using a balloon whisk, gradually mix the flour into the water until you have a smooth batter. Let stand for 15 minutes.

2 Heat enough oil to cover the bottom of a skillet over medium heat. To make small pancakes, pour a small quantity of batter into the skillet, or, if you prefer to make larger pancakes, swirl the skillet to spread the batter mixture. Cook one side for 3 minutes, then, using a spatula, turn over and cook the other side until golden. Keep warm while you repeat with the remaining batter to make 8 pancakes.

3 Meanwhile, to make the curry, put the carrots and potatoes into a steamer and steam until just tender but retaining some bite.

4 Heat the oil in a large, heavy-bottom pan over medium heat and add the cumin seeds, cardamom seeds, and mustard seeds. When they start to darken and sizzle, add the onions, partially cover, and cook over medium-low heat, stirring frequently, for 10 minutes, or until soft and golden.

5 Add the other spices, ginger, and garlic and cook, stirring constantly, for 1 minute. Add the strained tomatoes, stock, potatoes, and carrots, partially cover, and cook for 10–15 minutes, or until the vegetables are tender. Add the peas and spinach, then cook for an additional 2–3 minutes. Season to taste with salt before serving with the warm pancakes.

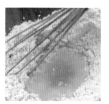

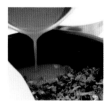

Nutritional Fact

Peas are a legume and therefore contain good levels of protein and soluble fiber to help maintain and clean out the bowel.

Serving Analysis

- Calories   467
- Protein   19g
- Carbohydrate   72g
- Sugars   5.9g
- Fat   14g
- Saturates   1.4g

serves 4

Spanish Tortilla

Ingredients

12 oz/350 g potatoes, cut into bite-size cubes
1 tbsp olive oil
1 tbsp dairy-free margarine
1 onion, thinly sliced
6 eggs, lightly beaten
salt and pepper

1 Cook the potatoes in a pan of salted boiling water for 10–12 minutes, or until tender. Drain well and set aside.

2 Meanwhile, heat the oil and margarine in a medium-size skillet with a heatproof handle over medium heat. Add the onion and cook, stirring occasionally, for 8 minutes, or until soft and golden. Add the potatoes and cook for an additional 5 minutes, stirring to prevent them sticking. Spread the onions and potatoes evenly over the bottom of the skillet.

3 Preheat the broiler to medium. Season the eggs to taste with salt and pepper and pour over the onion and potatoes. Cook over medium heat for 5–6 minutes, or until the eggs are just set and the base of the tortilla is lightly golden.

4 Place the skillet under the preheated broiler (if the handle is not heatproof, wrap with a double layer of foil) and cook the top of the tortilla for 2–3 minutes until it is just set and risen. Cut into wedges to serve.

Nutritional Fact
Potatoes are a good source of potassium, a highly beneficial mineral that helps the brain and nervous system to function.

Serving Analysis
- *Calories* — 254
- *Protein* — 11g
- *Carbohydrate* — 21g
- *Sugars* — 3g
- *Fat* — 143g
- *Saturates* — 2.8g

serves 4

Creamy Spinach & Mushroom Pasta

Ingredients

10¹/₂ oz/300 g dried gluten-free penne or pasta of your choice

salt and pepper

2 tbsp olive oil

9 oz/250 g mushrooms, sliced

1 tsp dried oregano

scant 1¹/₄ cups vegetable stock

1 tbsp lemon juice

6 tbsp vegan cream cheese

generous 1 cup frozen spinach leaves

Nutritional Fact
Spinach is high in potassium and folic acid and can help to reduce heart disease, eye degeneration, and the risk of cancer.

Serving Analysis
- *Calories* — 429
- *Protein* — 13g
- *Carbohydrate* — 61g
- *Sugars* — 2.2g
- *Fat* — 15g
- *Saturates* — 2.3g

1 Cook the pasta in a large pan of lightly salted boiling water according to the package instructions. Drain, reserving ³/₄ cup of the cooking liquid.

2 Meanwhile, heat the oil in a large, heavy-bottom skillet over medium heat, add the mushrooms, and cook, stirring frequently, for 8 minutes, or until almost crisp. Stir in the oregano, stock, and lemon juice and cook for 10–12 minutes, or until the sauce is reduced by half.

3 Stir in the cream cheese and spinach and cook over medium-low heat for 3–5 minutes. Add the reserved cooking liquid, then the cooked pasta. Stir well, season to taste with salt and pepper, and heat through before serving.

serves 4

Eggplant Tagine with Cornmeal

1 Preheat the broiler to medium. Toss the eggplant in 1 tablespoon of the oil and arrange in the broiler pan. Cook under the preheated broiler for 20 minutes, turning occasionally, until softened and starting to blacken around the edges—brush with more oil if the eggplant becomes too dry.

2 Heat the remaining oil in a large, heavy-bottom pan over medium heat. Add the onion and cook, stirring occasionally, for 8 minutes, or until soft and golden. Add the carrot, garlic, and mushrooms and cook for 5 minutes. Add the spices and cook, stirring constantly, for an additional minute.

3 Add the tomatoes and stock, stir well, then add the tomato paste. Bring to a boil, then reduce the heat and let simmer for 10 minutes, or until the sauce starts to thicken and reduce.

4 Add the eggplant, apricots, and chickpeas, partially cover, and cook for an additional 10 minutes, stirring occasionally.

5 Meanwhile, to make the cornmeal, pour the hot stock into a nonstick pan and bring to a boil. Pour in the cornmeal in a steady stream, stirring constantly with a wooden spoon. Reduce the heat to low and cook for 1–2 minutes, or until the cornmeal thickens to a mashed potatolike consistency. Serve the tagine with the cornmeal, sprinkled with the fresh cilantro.

Ingredients

1 eggplant, cut into $^1/_2$-inch/1-cm cubes

3 tbsp olive oil

1 large onion, thinly sliced

1 carrot, diced

2 garlic cloves, chopped

4 oz/115 g brown-cap mushrooms, sliced

2 tsp ground coriander

2 tsp cumin seeds

1 tsp chili powder

1 tsp ground turmeric

$2^1/_2$ cups canned chopped tomatoes

$1^1/_4$ cups vegetable stock

1 tbsp tomato paste

scant $^1/_2$ cup no-soak dried apricots, coarsely chopped

14 oz/400 g canned chickpeas, drained and rinsed

2 tbsp fresh cilantro, to garnish

For the cornmeal

5 cups hot vegetable stock

generous $^1/_4$ cup instant cornmeal

salt and pepper

makes 8

Thai Tofu Cakes with Chili Dip

Ingredients

10¹/₂ oz/300 g firm tofu (drained weight), coarsely grated

1 lemon grass stalk, outer layer discarded, finely chopped

2 garlic cloves, chopped

1-inch/2.5-cm piece fresh gingerroot, grated

2 kaffir lime leaves, finely chopped (optional)

2 shallots, finely chopped

2 fresh red chilies, seeded and finely chopped

4 tbsp chopped fresh cilantro

scant ²/₃ cup gluten-free all-purpose flour, plus extra for flouring

¹/₂ tsp salt

corn oil, for cooking

For the chili dip

3 tbsp white distilled vinegar or rice wine vinegar

2 scallions, finely sliced

1 tbsp superfine sugar

2 fresh chilies, finely chopped

2 tbsp chopped fresh cilantro

pinch of salt

Nutritional Fact
Tofu is a good source of protein that also contains B vitamins for energy and brain function and magnesium for calming the gut.

Serving Analysis
- *Calories*   130
- *Protein*   7.3g
- *Carbohydrate*   16g
- *Sugars*   4.3g
- *Fat*   4.9g
- *Saturates*   0.7g

1 To make the chili dip, mix all the ingredients together in a small serving bowl and set aside.

2 Mix the tofu with the lemon grass, garlic, ginger, lime leaves, if using, shallots, chilies, and cilantro in a mixing bowl. Stir in the flour and salt to make a coarse, sticky paste. Cover and let chill in the refrigerator for 1 hour to let the mixture firm up slightly.

3 Form the mixture into large walnut-size balls and, using floured hands, flatten into circles until you have 8 cakes. Heat enough oil to cover the bottom of a large, heavy-bottom skillet over medium heat. Cook the cakes in 2 batches, turning halfway through, for 4–6 minutes, or until golden brown. Drain on paper towels and serve warm with the chili dip.

serves 4

Roasted Butternut Squash Risotto

1 Preheat the oven to 400°F/200°C. Put the squash into a roasting pan.
Mix 1 tablespoon of the oil with the honey and spoon over the squash. Turn the
squash to coat it in the mixture. Roast in the preheated oven for 30–35 minutes,
or until tender.

2 Meanwhile, put the basil and oregano into a food processor with 2 tablespoons
of the remaining oil and process until finely chopped and blended. Set aside.

3 Heat the margarine and remaining oil in a large, heavy-bottom pan over medium
heat. Add the onions and cook, stirring occasionally, for 8 minutes, or until
soft and golden. Add the rice and cook for 2 minutes, stirring to coat the grains in
the oil mixture.

4 Pour in the wine and bring to a boil. Reduce the heat slightly and cook until the
wine is almost absorbed. Add the stock, a little at a time, and cook over medium-low
heat, stirring constantly, for 20 minutes.

5 Gently stir in the herb oil and squash until thoroughly mixed into the rice and cook
for an additional 5 minutes, or until the rice is creamy and cooked but retaining a
little bite in the center of the grain. Season well with salt and pepper before serving.

Nutritional Fact

*Butternut squash and
pumpkin are high in
the antioxidant beta-
carotene, which
protects against
damage from UV light.*

Serving Analysis
- Calories   436
- Protein   5.8g
- Carbohydrate   59g
- Sugars   9.3g
- Fat   17.5g
- Saturates   0.6g

Ingredients

1 lb 5 oz/600 g butternut squash
or pumpkin, peeled and cut into
bite-size pieces

4 tbsp olive oil

1 tsp honey

2 tbsp fresh basil

2 tbsp fresh oregano

1 tbsp dairy-free margarine

2 onions, finely chopped

1 lb/450 g risotto rice

3/4 cup dry white wine

5 cups vegetable stock

salt and pepper

Desserts & Baking

Delicious delights await you in this chapter. Sweet treats include rich, fudgy chocolate brownies, a sticky orange and almond cake, and a creamy mango baked cheesecake. Friends and family will be amazed that they are entirely wheat-, gluten-, and dairy-free. If you are looking for a healthy end to a meal, there's the refreshing pear and ginger granita.

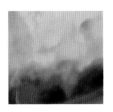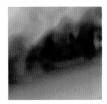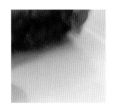

serves 4–6

Pear & Ginger Granita

Ingredients

scant $^1/_2$ cup superfine sugar

1 tbsp honey

scant 1 $^1/_4$ cups water

8 oz/225 g just-ripe pears, peeled, cored, and sliced

2 tsp finely chopped fresh gingerroot

3 tbsp lemon juice

1 Put the sugar, honey, and water into a pan over medium heat and heat, stirring, until the sugar has dissolved. Add the pears and ginger and let simmer for 5 minutes, then add the lemon juice.

2 Tip the pears and cooking liquid into a food processor or blender and process until almost smooth. Carefully pour the mixture into a freezerproof container with a lid and let cool.

3 Put in the freezer for 2 hours until the edges and bottom of the pear mixture are frozen. Remove the container from the freezer and mix with a fork so that the frozen part of the mixture is blended with the unfrozen part. Replace the lid and return to the freezer for an additional 1 $^1/_2$ hours.

4 Repeat the mixing process and freeze for an additional hour until the mixture forms ice crystals. Serve at this stage or return to the freezer until required, then remove 30 minutes before serving and mix with a fork. Serve spooned into glasses.

Nutritional Fact
Like apples, pears contain high levels of pectin, a type of fiber that is particularly good at carrying toxins out of the body and reducing blood cholesterol.

Serving Analysis
- *Calories*   *100*
- *Protein*   *0.2g*
- *Carbohydrate*   *26g*
- *Sugars*   *22g*
- *Fat*   *0.2g*
- *Saturates*   *0.01g*

serves 4

Apple & Plum Crumble

1 Preheat the oven to 350°F/180°C. Mix the apples, plums, apple juice, and sugar together in a 9-inch/23-cm round pie dish.

2 To make the topping, sift the flour into a mixing bowl and rub in the margarine with your fingertips until it resembles coarse bread crumbs. Stir in the buckwheat and rice flakes, sunflower seeds, sugar, and cinnamon, then spoon the topping over the fruit in the dish.

3 Bake the crumble in the preheated oven for 30–35 minutes, or until the topping is lightly browned and crisp.

Ingredients

4 apples, peeled, cored, and diced

5 plums, halved, pitted, and quartered

4 tbsp fresh apple juice

2 tbsp brown sugar

For the topping

generous ³/₄ cup gluten-free flour

2³/₄ oz/75 g dairy-free margarine, diced

generous ¹/₄ cup buckwheat flakes

generous ¹/₄ cup rice flakes

¹/₈ cup sunflower seeds

¹/₄ cup brown sugar

¹/₄ tsp ground cinnamon

Nutritional Fact
Apples and plums both release their sugars slowly and do not cause a sudden, undesirable rush of sugar into the bloodstream.

Serving Analysis

• Calories	495
• Protein	18g
• Carbohydrate	71g
• Sugars	43.5g
• Fat	19.5g
• Saturates	2.5g

serves 8

Chocolate Orange Mousse Cake

 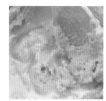 

1 Preheat the oven to 350°F/180°C. Grease a 9-inch/23-cm round, loose-bottom cake pan and line the bottom.

2 Cream the sugar and margarine together in a mixing bowl until pale and fluffy. Gradually add the eggs, beating well with a wooden spoon between each addition. Sift the flour, baking powder, and unsweetened cocoa together, fold half into the egg mixture, then fold in the remainder. Spoon the mixture into the prepared pan and level the surface with the back of a spoon. Bake in the preheated oven for 20 minutes until risen and firm to the touch. Leave in the pan to cool completely.

3 Meanwhile, melt the chocolate in a heatproof bowl placed over a pan of gently simmering water, making sure that the bottom of the bowl does not touch the water. Let cool, then stir in the orange rind and juice and the egg yolks.

4 Whisk the egg whites in a large bowl until they form stiff peaks. Gently fold a large spoonful of the egg whites into the chocolate mixture, then fold in the remainder. Spoon the mixture on top of the cooked, cooled sponge and level the top with the back of a spoon. Alternatively, remove the sponge from the tin, slice through, and sandwich with the mousse. Place in the refrigerator to set. Remove the sides of the pan if not removed before (though not the bottom) before decorating with the orange rind strips and serving.

Ingredients

$^1/_2$ cup superfine sugar

$3^1/_2$ oz/100 g dairy-free margarine, plus extra for greasing

2 eggs, lightly beaten

$^3/_4$ cup gluten-free all-purpose flour

1 tsp gluten-free baking powder

2 tbsp unsweetened cocoa

finely pared strips of orange rind, to decorate

For the mousse

7 oz/200 g good-quality semisweet chocolate (about 70 percent cocoa solids)

grated rind of 2 oranges and juice of 1

4 eggs, separated

Nutritional Fact
Chocolate contains catechins, which are antioxidant plant chemicals, similar to those found in fruits and vegetables.

Serving Analysis
- *Calories*   370
- *Protein*   7g
- *Carbohydrate*   38.5g
- *Sugars*   25g
- *Fat*   22.8g
- *Saturates*   8.4g

makes 12 brownies

Super Mocha Brownies

Ingredients

5½ oz/150 g good-quality semisweet chocolate (70 percent cocoa solids)

3½ oz/100 g dairy-free margarine, plus extra for greasing

1 tsp strong instant coffee

1 tsp vanilla extract

1 cup ground almonds

scant 1 cup superfine sugar

4 eggs, separated

confectioners' sugar, to decorate (optional)

Nutritional Fact

Semisweet chocolate contains more cocoa solids than milk chocolate, and has, therefore, more beneficial properties.

Serving Analysis

- *Calories*   254
- *Protein*   4.5g
- *Carbohydrate*   24g
- *Sugars*   20.5g
- *Fat*   17g
- *Saturates*   4.7g

1 Preheat the oven to 350°F/180°C. Grease an 8-inch/20-cm square cake pan and line the bottom.

2 Melt the chocolate and margarine in a heatproof bowl placed over a pan of gently simmering water, making sure that the bottom of the bowl does not touch the water. Stir very occasionally until the chocolate and margarine have melted and are smooth.

3 Carefully remove the bowl from the heat. Let cool slightly, then stir in the coffee and vanilla extract. Add the almonds and sugar and mix well until combined. Lightly beat the egg yolks in a separate bowl, then stir into the chocolate mixture.

4 Whisk the egg whites in a large bowl until they form stiff peaks. Gently fold a large spoonful of the egg whites into the chocolate mixture, then fold in the remainder until completely incorporated.

5 Spoon the mixture into the prepared pan and bake in the preheated oven for 35–40 minutes, or until risen and firm on top but still slightly gooey in the center. Let cool in the pan, then turn out, remove the lining paper, and cut into 12 pieces. Dust with confectioners' sugar before serving, if liked.

serves 8

Mango & Maple Cheesecake

Ingredients

2¹/₂ oz/70 g dairy-free margarine, plus extra for greasing

6 oz/175 g gluten- and dairy-free cookies, such as digestives, crushed

generous ³/₈ cup ground almonds

For the filling

1 large mango, seeded, peeled, and diced

juice of 1 lemon

scant 1 cup plain soy yogurt

1 tbsp gluten-free cornstarch

3 tbsp maple syrup

1 lb/450 g vegan cream cheese

For the topping

3 tbsp maple syrup

1 small mango, seeded, peeled, and sliced

1 Preheat the oven to 350°F/180°C. Lightly grease a 9-inch/23-cm round, loose-bottom cake pan. To make the cookie base, melt the margarine in a medium-size pan, then stir in the crushed cookies and almonds. Then press the mixture into the bottom of the prepared cake pan to make an even layer. Bake in the preheated oven for 10 minutes.

2 Meanwhile, to make the filling, put the mango, lemon juice, yogurt, cornstarch, maple syrup, and cream cheese into a food processor or blender and process until smooth and creamy. Pour the mixture over the cookie base and level with the back of a spoon. Bake for 25–30 minutes, or until golden and set. Let cool in the pan, then transfer to a wire rack and let chill in the refrigerator for 30 minutes to firm up.

3 To make the topping, heat the maple syrup in a skillet. Brush the top of the cheesecake with the maple syrup. Add the mango to the remaining maple syrup in the skillet and cook for 1 minute, stirring. Let cool slightly, then arrange the mango slices on top of the cheesecake. Pour over any remaining syrup before serving.

Nutritional Fact

Mangoes are a rich source of beta-carotene and other carotenoids, the plant chemicals that provide their rich golden color and help to protect the body.

Serving Analysis

- Calories   464
- Protein   8g
- Carbohydrate   35g
- Sugars   22g
- Fat   34.5g
- Saturates   4g

makes 9 slices

Orange & Almond Syrup Cake

Ingredients

dairy-free margarine, for greasing

6 eggs, separated

1 cup superfine sugar

grated rind of 3 oranges

generous 1 1/2 cups ground almonds

For the topping

juice of 3 oranges

3 tbsp honey

Nutritional Fact
Almonds help to balance blood sugar and so when they are used in a sweet dish, they help to dilute the effects of a sudden rush of sugar.

Serving Analysis
- Calories   269
- Protein   7.9g
- Carbohydrate   34g
- Sugars   30g
- Fat   12.3g
- Saturates   1.8g

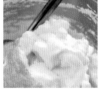

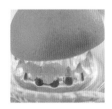

1 Preheat the oven to 350°F/180°C. Grease an 8-inch/20-cm square cake pan and line the bottom. Beat the egg yolks with the sugar, orange rind, and almonds in a large mixing bowl.

2 Whisk the egg whites in a separate large bowl until they form stiff peaks. Fold a spoonful of the egg whites into the almond mixture, then fold in the remainder. Carefully pour the mixture into the prepared cake pan.

3 Bake in the preheated oven for 45–50 minutes, or until a skewer inserted into the center of the cake comes out clean. Let cool in the pan.

4 To make the topping, put the orange juice and honey into a small pan and bring to a boil, stir once, then cook, without stirring, for 6–8 minutes, or until reduced, thickened, and syrupy. Using a fork, pierce the cake all over, then pour the syrup over the top and let soak in before serving.

makes 12

Banana Muffins with Cinnamon Frosting

Ingredients

generous 1 cup gluten-free all-purpose flour

1 tsp gluten-free baking powder

pinch of salt

generous $^3/_4$ cup superfine sugar

6 tbsp dairy-free milk

2 eggs, lightly beaten

$5^1/_2$ oz/150 g dairy-free margarine, melted

2 small bananas, mashed

For the frosting

scant $^1/_4$ cup vegan cream cheese

2 tbsp dairy-free margarine

$^1/_4$ tsp ground cinnamon

scant 1 cup confectioners' sugar

Nutritional Fact

Cinnamon, like almonds, helps to balance blood sugar and reduce the ill-effects of sweet foods.

Serving Analysis

• Calories	272
• Protein	2.7g
• Carbohydrate	34g
• Sugars	22g
• Fat	14.5g
• Saturates	2.8g

1 Preheat the oven to 400°F/200°C. Place 12 large paper cases in a deep muffin pan. Sift the flour, baking powder, and salt together into a mixing bowl. Stir in the sugar.

2 Whisk the milk, eggs, and margarine together in a separate bowl until combined. Slowly stir into the flour mixture without beating. Fold in the mashed bananas.

3 Spoon the mixture into the paper cases and bake in the preheated oven for 20 minutes until risen and golden. Turn out onto a wire rack and let cool.

4 To make the frosting, beat the cream cheese and margarine together in a bowl, then beat in the cinnamon and confectioners' sugar until smooth and creamy. Chill the frosting in the refrigerator for about 15 minutes to firm up, then top each muffin with a spoonful.

makes one 1 lb/450 g loaf

Red Bell Pepper Cornbread

Nutritional Fact

Red bell peppers contain the chemical capsaicin, which is thought to soothe the pain of indigestion.

Serving Analysis

- Calories   104
- Protein   5.9g
- Carbohydrate   12.2g
- Sugars   0.9g
- Fat   4g
- Saturates   0.3g

Ingredients

1 large red bell pepper, seeded and sliced

1 1/8 cups fine cornmeal

scant 7/8 cup gluten-free white bread flour

1 tbsp gluten-free baking powder

1 tsp salt

2 tsp sugar

scant 1 1/4 cups dairy-free milk

2 eggs, lightly beaten

3 tbsp olive oil, plus extra for oiling

1 Preheat the oven to 400°F/200°C. Lightly oil a 1 lb/450 g loaf pan. Arrange the red bell pepper slices on a baking sheet and roast in the preheated oven for 35 minutes until tender and the skin starts to blister. Set aside to cool slightly, then peel away the skin.

2 Meanwhile, mix the cornmeal, flour, baking powder, salt, and sugar together in a large mixing bowl. Beat the milk, eggs, and oil together in a separate bowl or pitcher and gradually add to the flour mixture. Beat with a wooden spoon to make a thick, smooth, batterlike consistency.

3 Finely chop the red bell pepper and fold into the cornmeal mixture, then spoon into the prepared pan. Bake in the preheated oven for 30 minutes until lightly golden. Leave in the pan for 10 minutes, then run a knife around the edge of the pan and turn the loaf out onto a wire rack to cool. To keep fresh, wrap the loaf in foil or seal in a plastic bag.

Index